Desirée Mays

Opera Unveiled

2007

[signature: Desirée Mays]

♪

ART FORMS INC.
Santa Fe · Salt Lake City

ISBN 978-0-9707822-6-7

To order individual copies of *Opera Unveiled 1999 - 2007*
please send a check for $17 (postage included) to:
Art Forms, Inc., 31 Valencia Loop
Santa Fe, New Mexico 87508
Fax: (505) 466 1908
Email: dmmays@gmail.com

Contents

La Bohème

Giacomo Puccini

"*I* am the poet, she is the poetry" (Son io il poeta, essa la poesia), Rodolfo sings of the consumptive Mimi in a line that pretty well sums up Giacomo Puccini's approach to most of his operas: "I am the composer, and you, my suffering heroine, are my Muse, my inspiration."

Giacomo Puccini labored greatly in giving birth to the children of his imagination. Once a source had been chosen, he vacillated back and forth over the libretto, pushing his librettists, in this case Luigi Illica and Giuseppe Giacosa, to the limits with his constant changes. After Puccini insisted that Giacosa, a respected poet, playwright, and author, change one section of *La Bohème* five times, Giacosa wrote a letter of resignation to Giulio Ricordi, the music publisher who had commissioned the work. Only Ricordi's delicate diplomacy brought Giacosa back to the fold. Part of the problem was that Puccini attempted something entirely new with *La Bohème*; he was writing, not about historic characters who lived in other places at other times, but about real people, about operatically deprived people, many of whom may well have been living in the attics surrounding the theatre in which patrons sat watching the opera. There was nothing glamorous about the struggling artists in *La Bohème*.

This realistic perspective was not helped by the fact that the first performances of *La Bohème* were held as part of a season that also offered the Italian premieres of Wagner's *Götterdämmerung*, and Verdi's final opera, *Falstaff*, both new and highly successful works that easily overshadowed Puccini's simple, girl-next-door story. What a shift from the grandeur of the final opera of Wagner's Ring cycle or the Shakespearian magnificence of Falstaff to the freezing attic studio of four out-of-work artists and their provocative girlfriends! Morever, Puccini was mixing comedy with tragedy, something that was never done; opera at the time was either *seria* or *buffa*, tragic or comic. First-night audiences at Turin's Teatro Reggio in 1896 were surprised, not sure how to respond to these contemporary ideas. The critics, on the whole, were not positive. The public, however, people of the industrial cities of northern Italy, soon responded enthusiastically, and *La Bohème* quickly became a major success.

With *La Bohème*, his fourth opera, Puccini was getting into his stride and understood well his craft and the direction that his operas would take. His first two, *Le Villi* and *Edgar*, works of an inexperienced composer, were followed by *Manon Lescaut*, in which he refined the characterization of his protagonists and the music that described them. In *La Bohème* he finds his path, telling opera tales as "tragedies of fragile sentiment." Pathos becomes a major component of his work.

Puccini was 36 years old when he wrote *La Bohème*, and his own time of personal struggle was not so far behind him that he did not remember vividly the trials and joys of those capricious days of youth. One of eight children, Puccini was raised by his mother, Albina, following his father's death when Giacomo was five. Coming from many generations of highly respected cathedral organists, Puccini was expected to continue in the family tradition but, at an early age, decided that church music was not for him; instead he wanted to compose operas. His mother was his major support, even writing a letter entreating Queen Margherita for a grant to enable Giacomo to study music at the Milan Conservatory. Mother and son scratched funds together, and Giacomo set off for Milan in 1880. Although not an exemplary student, he learned his craft. He had very little money in those days and shared an apartment with Pietro Mascagni, who later composed *Cavalleria Rusticana*. Puccini's first compositions met with little success until Giulio Ricordi, director of Italy's most important music publishing house, recognized his potential and signed him up. *Le Villi* was the first product of their collaboration. Ricordi stood by Puccini through the difficulties of those first operas, never losing faith in the young composer's talent.

In March 1893, Puccini ran into his friend, Leoncavallo, who had just become famous with his opera *I Pagliacci*. Leoncavallo informed Puccini that he was working on a libretto based on a book by Henri Murger called *Scènes de la Vie de Bohème*. Puccini, who was very competitive, replied that he too was working on the same piece. This would not be the first time Puccini would work on the same text as another composer. Previously, both he and Massenet had presented their own versions of *Manon*, Massenet in 1884 and Puccini in 1893. Now, Puccini's response to an angry Leoncavallo was printed in the newspaper: "Let him compose, and I shall compose, and the public will judge." A few years later, aided and abetted by Ricordi, Puccini took the libretto of *Tosca* away from an unsuspecting composer, Franchetti, by very questionable means in order to compose his own version.

Given his personal experience as a poverty-stricken music student, it is easy to understand why Puccini was drawn to *Scènes de la Vie de Bohème*. Set in Paris in the 1830s, the book, written in a series of unrelated prose sketches, portrayed the

Bohemian way of life. Henri Murger, its author, described those days as "A charming life, yet a terrible one." Puccini was drawn to the strong characters of the four young artists and their two lady loves, and saw potential in the action he found in the book. The transition from book to a coherent libretto was difficult; it took three tempestuous years of writing and revision before Puccini was satisfied with the final libretto. Giacosa wrote the verses while Illica structured the scenes and outlines, their roles often overlapping. Though Puccini did not write himself, he had a very clear understanding and an instinctive sense of what would or would not work in the theatre. He was breaking new ground with *La Bohème*, a point of ongoing friction with his librettists. In spite of the difficulties, however, after Giacosa heard the music that had been composed to his verses, he wrote to Ricordi, "Puccini has surpassed all my expectations, and I now understand the reason for his tyranny over verses and accents." The two librettists went on to write two more libretti for their difficult composer: *Madama Butterfly* and *Tosca*.

The term "Bohemian" did not refer directly to the country Bohemia, as one might expect, but was rather a synonym for gypsies, people who had come from the east. By the mid-19th century, "Bohemians" described the impoverished artists and students who lived in the Latin Quarter of Paris, young people who were unconventional, resisting bourgeois respectability, a counterculture. It was Henri Murger, himself a member of this culture, who placed the word "Bohemian" firmly into the vocabulary in the mid 1840s, first in his articles on Bohemian life, then in the play based on the articles and finally in his book *Scènes de la Vie de Bohème*. He stated in the opening chapter: "The stories are only, in reality, studies of manners, and their heroes belong to a class misjudged up to now, whose greatest fault is disorder, yet they excuse this disorder as a necessity which life demands from them." Theirs was an easy-come, easy-go existence peppered with good humor. In the book, when the landlord, upon seeing no bed in the attic room, asks Marcel what he sleeps on, he is told, "On a good conscience, sir."

Both book and opera are rooted in the lives of four friends: Rodolfe (Rodolfo), Marcel (Marcello), Colline, and Schaunard. While Rodolfo may be Murger himself, the others were modeled on friends from his youth when they all shared a Bohemian way of life in Paris. Known as the Four Musketeers, Murger and his friends hung out at the Café Momus (which really existed), drank copious cups of coffee, and drove away the Café's normal patrons with their outrageous chatter and carryings-on. The first article Murger wrote about this lifestyle, the love between Rodolfe, a poet, and a girlfriend, was a thinly disguised autobiographical account of Murger's actual encounter with one Lucile, a seamstress of silk flowers.

In the opera the four friends are young men with lofty dreams and high aspirations. Rodolfo tells Mimi he is a poet and a dreamer: "In dreams and fond illusions, no-one is richer than I." When he meets Mimi and falls in love with her, he sees her as the manifestation of his dreams. She is as beautiful as the dawn, he tells her, adoring her tiny hands, and awed by the sight of her pale face "wreathed in moonlight." In his first aria, the famous "Che gelida manina" (Your tiny hand is frozen), Rodolfo impetuously pours out his heart to his unexpected visitor. He writes articles, but barely makes a living at it. He has written a play, but when the cold becomes unbearable in the attic studio, he burns his play page by page for warmth, egged on by his equally cold and hungry friends who find the burning play "sparkling," then "too short in its phrases," as the flames die away. The musical score graphically describes the fire as it flares up, dances merrily along, then slowly dies as the drama feeding it crackles, curls up, and dies.

Marcello is a painter, a baritone, a close and true friend

to Rodolfo. He has been struggling with his painting "The Passage of the Red Sea" for some time now, submitting it to various galleries and museums without success. By the third act he is forced to sell his great work, which becomes a sign hung outside a tavern. This was not what he had envisioned for himself.

Schaunard, another baritone, is a musician. In the opening scene he provides a feast for his friends, with wine and cigars as well as wood for the stove. As they unpack the food and wine, he explains how he acquired these provisions: an Englishman offered him a large sum of money if he would play music until a parrot, who was driving the Englishman crazy, died. Schaunard played and played for three days, but nothing happened, the bird continued to hold forth in full voice. So Schaunard devised a plan: he flirted with the maid of the bird's owner, and together they managed to kill the bird when it choked on a sprig of parsley. The Englishman paid up, and Schaunard went shopping.

Colline, a bass, is a philosopher, mildly eccentric and not as old as he is typically portrayed; all four of these young men are in their 20s. They share their triumphs and failures, their hunger and their dreams. Colline owns a long overcoat with four cavernous pockets, each one named for a different public library in Paris. The pockets of the great coat are filled at all times with his books. Colline frequently quotes the classics; these are, after all, an educated if impoverished group of young men.

At the start of the opera, it is Christmas Eve, and Marcello and Rodolfo are at work painting and writing. The four friends gather in a freezing attic that overlooks the snowy rooftops of Paris. They decide to burn Rodolfo's play in the stove to keep themselves warm. Colline enters and joins in the burning of the play. Then Schaunard arrives with the feast, and the exuberance of the four infects the music as they laugh together, although Schaunard is slightly annoyed because no-one pays any attention to his tale of the parrot. There is a knock at the door. It is the landlord, wanting his rent. He is described by Murger as "M. Benoit [who] exhaled a pestilent odour of bad brandy and unpaid rent." They invite him in, give him some wine, and then make fun of his habit of flirting with young girls. Pretending mock indignation at this unseemly behavior, the friends push him out the door and prepare to go out into the streets of the Latin Quarter to celebrate Christmas Eve. Rodolfo stays behind to put the finishing touches to an article he is writing for "The Beaver."

Hearing a timid knock at the door, Rodolfo opens it to reveal the young woman who lives upstairs. Her candle has blown out. He invites her in. She is beautiful, but pale, and appears to be ill. He sits her down by the fire and pours her a glass of wine to warm her up. She revives, attempts to leave, but drops her key. The candles blow out, and the young pair get down on the floor in the dark searching for the key. Rodolfo's hand finds Mimi's; her tiny hand is frozen. Thus begins the famous tenor aria in which he tells her about himself. He sings of his dreams and how enraptured he is by her eyes. She responds with her own meltingly lovely aria, "Mi chiamano Mimi" (They call me Mimi). She is a seamstress, she explains, and in her attic room she embroiders flowers that speak to her of love and springtime. She lives simply throughout the cold winter, waiting for the first kiss of spring.

Then, thinking she has said too much, she apologizes for her intrusion. Neither wants to part, and when Schaunard and the others call Rodolfo to hurry and join them, he replies that he is bringing a friend. He then turns and sees Mimi in the moonlight and passionately avows his love for her. Mimi timidly draws near and then, arm in arm, singing ecstatically of their love, they leave the stage together.

Act II opens with a lively street scene, seething with crowds of people milling about in the frosty night air.

Rodolfo buys Mimi a pink bonnet that complements her dark hair, then introduces her to his friends. Together they all sit down to dine at the Café Momus. They are in the midst of ordering a lavish meal, when a commotion is heard in the street: Musetta has arrived, followed by Alcindoro, a pompous old gentlemen, bearing luxurious packages. Musetta is a singer, coquettish, vivacious, and the love of Marcello's life. He pales when he sees her, telling the others how she "varies her love and her lovers without number." Seeing Marcello turn away from her, Musetta at once occupies a nearby table, with Alcindoro in tow. She sings her famous waltz song about the joy of life, and how she enjoys all the attention she attracts. She flirts with Marcello, and it doesn't take long for him to succumb. Suddenly she lets out a shriek: her shoe is hurting her, Alcindoro must go at once and get it fixed. Once he has gone, she and Marcello throw their arms around one another. The bill for the meal arrives and there is consternation. The friends cannot pay it. Musetta has an idea; she orders the waiter to put the bill on Alcindoro's table, and then she and the others leave, dancing amongst the crowd to the music of a military band.

Act III opens two months later at the Barrière d'Enfer, one of gates into the city of Paris. The librettists give specific stage instructions as to how this scene should appear in the "misty gloom of February in the dim light of early dawn with the toll-gate on one side of the stage and a tavern with Marcello's painting hung as a sign out front on the other." The music evokes falling snow in a descending motif of parallel fifths on harp and flute. Officers open the gates and the people, many bearing farm produce, pour in. The tavern is brightly lit, and sounds of Musetta's laughter can be heard coming from inside. Mimi appears, coughing in the cold air. She asks a servant to tell Marcello that she waits for him outside the inn.

Marcello, surprised to see her, tells Mimi that he and

Musetta are staying at the tavern, where Musetta teaches singing while he paints signs. Mimi tells him why she has come. She and Rodolfo are not getting along because he is jealous of her every move. The night before, she goes on, they had a row, and Rodolfo left her and went to the tavern. She wants Marcello to help them separate, but she refuses to see Rodolfo herself. Marcello tells her gently to go home, then turns to meet Rodolfo as he emerges from the tavern. Mimi quickly hides.

Rodolfo tells his friend that he too wants to part from Mimi, whom he accuses of flirting with every man she meets. Marcello chides him, "That's not true!" Rodolfo sadly agrees and owns up. He loves Mimi, he confesses, but fears for her because she is so sickly, her coughing never ceases. He believes she is dying and blames himself for not being able to provide for her; their home is squalid, cold. His frustration with the situation expresses itself in anger. Mimi, coughing, gives away her hiding place and Rodolfo runs to her, horrified that she has heard his conversation with Marcello. He tries to comfort her. Peals of laughter are heard from inside the tavern and Marcello rushes off, furious with Musetta who, he is certain, is flirting with the customers.

Mimi sings a sad farewell to Rodolfo, "Addio, addio senza rancor" (Goodbye, with no hard feelings). In this plaintive aria, the music follows the vocal line, making it doubly poignant. Mimi will return to her lonely existence. She asks that he collect her few belongings and she will have them picked up. She suggests he keep the little bonnet as a memento of their love. The heartbroken Rodolfo kisses her goodbye, but then, finding themselves incapable of parting, they agree to stay together until "springtime brings glorious sunshine!" From inside the tavern Marcello and Musetta can be heard arguing heatedly, and a lively quartet ensues in which the tender words of love between Rodolfo and Mimi are sung above a stream of invective from Marcello and

Musetta. Musetta storms off as Rodolfo and Mimi leave the stage together.

The final act of *La Bohème* is set some months later. Marcello and Rodolfo are once again sharing the attic apartment. Pretending to work, they are dreaming instead of their lost loves: Musetta has been seen riding in a carriage, and Mimi was seen dressed like a duchess. Although they pretend not to mind, both men are suffering. Schaunard and Colline arrive with a meager supper – four rolls and a small herring, which is later divided into four tiny pieces. (Apparently, once when Puccini and Mascagni were students and very low on funds, they too once shared a single herring for dinner.) The four musketeers treat this tiny meal as if it were a royal banquet. Then, to warm themselves, they dance and end up fighting a mock duel.

Suddenly Musetta appears at the door, very upset. "It's Mimi, she's very ill and has collapsed trying to climb the stairs." Mimi is dying; her consumption, exacerbated by poverty, cold, and malnutrition, has nearly run its course. Rodolfo runs to help, leads her in, and gently lays her on the bed. The others stand around, not sure what to do. Happy to see her friends, Mimi greets them all; she has come to be near Rodolfo and explains how Musetta has befriended her. One by one the friends decide how they can best help. Mimi's hands are cold, she wants her muff. Musetta takes off her earrings and gives them to Marcello, saying, "Let's sell them and buy a muff." They leave together. Taking off his great overcoat, Colline sings a sad aria of farewell, for he plans to sell it to buy medicine. There is irony in this overly heartfelt aria as Colline bids farewell, not only to his overcoat and by extension to Mimi, but perhaps to the Bohemian way of life as well. Schaunard leaves with him.

At last alone, Rodolfo and Mimi renew their vows of love, recalling their first meeting in this very room as all the early musical motifs come flooding back with their memories. The friends return with their gifts, Musetta kneels to pray to the Virgin, and Mimi falls asleep. Mercifully, Puccini at this point does not require a tour de force aria from his dying Mimi; instead she simply closes her eyes, her breathing stills, and she slips away, surrounded by the people she loves. Rodolfo leaves for a moment to pull the shade over the window as his friends realize that Mimi has died. Rodolfo senses a change and, in spoken words, demands of his friends, "Why do you look at me like that?" The music pauses, there is silence, and everything is still until Marcello steps forward and, embracing Rodolfo, urges "Coraggio!" (Courage!). The music returns with great forte chords, Rodolfo collapses onto the bed crying "Mimi! Mimi!" as the curtain slowly falls.

Although delicate in its sentiments, Puccini composed music for *La Bohème* that was written with such passion and awareness of the dramatic requirements that the opera has remained irresistible for over 100 years. His blending of comic with dramatic moments is both brilliant and heart-wrenching; we see in the first act the antics of the young men followed by a swift shift into deeply touching arias followed in turn by a yearning love duet. Musetta's naughtiness in the Christmas Eve scene is balanced masterfully by the tearing poignancy of the cold morning scene at the Barrière d'Enfer. Humor returns with pathos as the friends try, in the last act, to make the best of things, of their losses, of their slim meal, in their play-acting. Humor is interrupted by tragedy with Musetta's announcement that Mimi is dying on the doorstep.

Puccini contrasts irony and true emotion throughout the work, the pretended gaiety when the artists are not doing well, the mock solemnity, the teasing of the landlord when they too would like to be enjoying the company of pretty girls, the whole Bohemian outlook on life. The two women are deliberately contrasted: the touching formality of Mimi is set against the flamboyance of Musetta, the sweet tenderness of Mimi's love against the high excitement of Musetta's.

Both Mimi and Musetta represent young, single women with few resources at the time of Louis Napoleon. Musetta was a glamorous singer who passed easily from one rich lover to the next; as long as they acceded to her every whim, she kept them amused. The man she cannot forget is Marcello, who has nothing to offer her materially, yet she keeps coming back to him, only to leave again. Their tempestuous relationship seems to thrive on never knowing what the next day will bring. To Mimi, however, Musetta is a good friend. They quickly take to each other at their first meeting at the Café Momus. When both women have gone their different ways with new lovers, Musetta keeps in touch with Mimi and comes to her rescue when she is in real need, bringing her to their friends at the end.

Mimi ekes out a living as a seamstress, making beautiful imitation flowers for the silk textile industry. Before meeting Rodolfo, hers was a lonely existence in a bare room with no heating and little food. Many such women lived in these poor circumstances, and many succumbed to tuberculosis. After leaving Rodolfo, Mimi does indeed becomes the mistress of a wealthy man who pays for her dresses and keeps her warm at least. But she cannot be happy in such a situation for she truly loves Rodolfo.

Young working-class women such as Mimi and Musetta were called grisettes, a word derived from the cheap gray *(gris)* material of the dresses they wore. They enjoyed an easy lifestyle similar to their Bohemian male counterparts. Typically they had jobs that paid subsistence wages; they welcomed the attentions of men who could improve their situation, but they were proud of their independence. In 19th-century Paris they became associated with the Latin Quarter, where housing was cheap. They provided romance, inspiration, and an audience for their would-be artist lovers. Their primary aim was to find security, preferably in marriage to a man of the bourgeois or upper class. If they did not find a husband while their beauty lasted, they might face prostitution, consumption, and a lonely death. They had little education, but were intelligent, bright, and above all, attractive. Grisettes flirted outrageously and insisted on a relationship of equality with their lovers, Bohemian or otherwise.

Puccini was drawn to such women all his life, both personally and in his operas. As a student familiar with a Bohemian lifestyle, he was able to depict women both frivolous and suffering. Women like Manon, Musetta, and even Tosca, loved to be center stage, to be admired and feted, while Puccini's vulnerable heroines – Madama Butterfly, Mimi, Liù – suffered for love. The heroines Puccini adored provided him with his greatest inspiration, and typically he made them pay the ultimate price of dying for love. Unlike Wagner and Verdi, with their larger-than-life heroines, Puccini depicted women not as mythic characters but as people we know and with whom we can identify: the little seamstress, the servant girl, the singer who lives for art and love, even as Puccini did. These were the women of his creative imagination for whom he composed music that is remarkable, heartfelt, and sensitive, with action that is swift, naturalistic, and flowing, accompanied by romantic rhetoric that rarely fails to appeal.

While the opera ends with Mimi's death, Henri Murger takes us forward in time to learn what becomes of the four friends who collectively leave their Bohemian lifestyle behind, go their separate ways, and join the bourgeoisie, conforming to a more or less conventional lifestyle: Rodolfe "came before the public eye with a book [*Scènes de la Vie Bohème!*] that had the critics' attention for a month." Schaunard published a book of songs that established his reputation; Marcel finally sold some paintings to the Salon, including one to a rich Englishman who had been Musetta's lover; while Colline "made an advantageous marriage; he gave parties with music and cake." Musetta married a postmaster. "The past is dead and buried," Marcel points out at the end of the book, "We are only young once."

♪

Characters

Rodolfo, a poet	tenor
Marcello, a painter	baritone
Colline, a philosopher	bass
Schaunard, a musician	baritone
Mimi, a seamstress	soprano
Musetta, a singer	soprano

Bibliography

Carner, Mosco. *Puccini: A Critical Biography*. New York: Alfred A. Knopf, 1959.

John, Nicholas, ed. *La Bohème*, English National Opera Guide 14. New York: Riverrun Press Inc., 1982.

Lee, M. Owen. *First Intermissions*. Oxford: Oxford University Press, Inc., 1995.

Murger, Henri. *La Bohème: Scènes de la Vie de Bohème*. Salt Lake City: Peregrine Smith Books, 1988.

Osborne, Charles. *The Complete Operas of Puccini*. New York: Da Capo Press, 1988.

Stanley, Sadie, ed. *The New Grove Dictionary of Opera*, Vol.3. London: MacMillan Reference Ltd., 1998.

Tea:
A Mirror of Soul

Tan Dun

In *Tea: A Mirror of Soul*, the opera theatre is changed into a great tea house into which we, the audience, are invited to enter as honored guests in a magical space. Composer Tan Dun has transformed the tea ceremony and the music of his land, China, into a shared experience of different cultures, traditions, and above all, music. As we are drawn into this unique work we experience a deep sense of tranquillity and peace. Tan Dun's global vision presents what can truly be described as a total experience of music theatre in a new century.

In keeping with Taoist tradition, nature is an integral part of his opera, with stones, water, and ceramic, the clays of the earth, introduced in the percussion. Even paper plays a role. Hanging from the flies above the stage in great sheets, the paper rustles back and forth in the moving air. Following the premiere of *Tea* in 2002, the *Tokyo Journal* reported, "Water, stone, earth and paper are brought into surprising harmony with the orchestra, creating magical effects. Their sounds cross the borders of time and cultural differences, and touch the essence of human life. The various instruments, themes and voices refer to music of many periods and modern peoples, including Chinese, Japanese and European; all of these influences are filtered by Tan Dun and brought into a perfect harmony that is characteristic of all his music."

Tea will have a special resonance at The Santa Fe Opera, whose theatre is open to the high-desert terrain and the sky with its sunsets, storms, and moonlit nights. Paper may take on a life all its own in this setting, as the night breezes drift across the stage.

Written by composer Tan Dun and Xu Ying, a playwright at the Chinese National Theatre, the story and music are, Tan Dun says, "inspired by the proclamation chants of Japanese and Tibetan priests, the recitation methods of Chinese poetry and vocal techniques from Noh, classical Chinese opera and from the lyrical styles of European opera. [The libretto] was written poetically in my own words."

Tea is a simple tale about the love of a young prince and princess, a brother and sister, whose lives change when Seikyo, a Japanese prince, arrives and expresses his love for the princess Lan. The two princes argue over the validity of a special book called *The Book of Tea*. Seikyo contends that the brother's copy is a fraud and declares that he will go, with Lan, to seek the original book. Each man vows to sacrifice his life to the one who finds the true book.

Lan and Seikyo journey far to find Luyu, the master sage and author of *The Book of Tea*. They find only Luyu's daughter, Lu, who gives the book to them. The jealous prince arrives, a fight ensues, and Lan, caught in the middle, dies by her brother's sword. The prince offers his life to Seikyo, who chooses not to take revenge. Seikyo returns to Japan and joins a temple for the rest of his days.

This triangular love story is not complicated, but the manner in which it is told is a challenge of a special kind. Addressing the fundamental elements of human life: love, philosophy, emotions, tradition, religion, and nature, Tan

Dun has blended abstraction and reality, complexity and simplicity, symbol and metaphor.

The opera opens in a Japanese temple in ninth-century Kyoto. The silence is slowly filled by the sound of water as it is lifted ritualistically from a clear glass bowl by the hands of a young woman, then allowed to drip back into the bowl through her fingers. A single voice intones the sound of "Om." Nine monks in long robes chant as they conduct a tea ceremony with slow reverence; the sound of their bass-baritone voices is deep, sonorous, hypnotic. The high monk, Seikyo, raises an empty bowl to his lips, savoring empty tea, recalling the times when he drank tea with Lan: "To hear the color, to see the sound, to drink tea with Lan, not for thirst, but for feeling the warmth, touching inner space." The monks did not know their master was a prince. He begins to tell them his story, accompanied by the sound of water slapping rhythmically in the bowl. "It was ten years ago," Seikyo begins.

The scene shifts imperceptibly to a palace in Chang'an, the ancient capital of China. Princess Lan and her brother, the Prince, are acting a shadow play called "The Monkey King," for their father, the Emperor. Their play is stylized, ritualistic, the movements prescribed. Playing the part of the Monkey King, the Prince sings to the sister he loves, "Without you, life is living death," while the nine bass-baritones bound about the stage as a chorus of monkeys. The Emperor is delighted by his children's play.

Seikyo enters and the play comes to a halt. The Emperor asks what brings him to the palace. Years earlier he and Lan had met and exchanged promises, and now he has returned to claim her. Lan is joyful, her brother furious and mistrustful, the Emperor uncertain. He asks Seikyo, in the tradition of the court of the Tang Dynasty, to compose a poem for Lan and chooses the theme of tea, a highly revered subject. Seikyo at once composes a poem:

> *tea –*
> *sensual green,*
> *a watery beauty.*
> *up-floating dreams,*
> *down-sinking leaves,*
> *if one desires to live forever,*
> *taste a thick and light bowl of tea.*

The Emperor then requests a verse in couplets, and Seikyo complies. The Emperor is satisfied, the Prince infuriated: "If you would take my sister, you first break my heart with a sword." The Emperor calls the Lady of Ritual to prepare the tea ceremony which, in China, involves much movement, color, and sound; insistent gongs, bells, and chimes express the feelings between the princess and her lover.

The ceremony is interrupted by the announcement that there is a stranger at the gates; the Prince of Persia offers one thousand horses in exchange for a book. The Emperor asks about this book. "It is," the Ritualist tells him, "a book of wisdom with thousands of treasured secrets, fire crosses water, Yin and Yang, lines map the inner spaces of body and mind." The Prince, Lan's brother, announces that he has the book; he and Lan have studied the Tao of tea together from its pages, he hands the book to his father. Seikyo is skeptical and says the book is a fraud. He insists that he knows the true author of *The Book of Tea*: Luyu, the sage of tea. The book is very valuable. The furious Prince challenges Seikyo: "If you can show me this sage, I will lay my life at your feet." Seikyo accepts the challenge, and agrees that whoever finds the true book will hold forfeit the life of the other. Lan despairs that the two men she loves are ready to sacrifice their lives for a book, but both are resolute. Her weeping is heard over the chanting of the monks as the first act ends.

In Act II, shadowed images come into focus, revealing silhouetted bodies moving as in an erotic dream. Lan and Seikyo tenderly express their love for one another – in the language of tea.

Lan: *sweet,*
         as petals,
         brushing lips,
         arousing the mind,
         savor first the bitterness.
         then, wait: the surging flood.
         warm as breath, light as wings,
         kissed by pale and tenderest moon,
         dancing with head thrown back.
         tea, whence do you come?
         shimmering dreams,
         fallen leaves,
         seed.

Through the long months of searching for Luyu, their love has grown and they hope that, over time, the Prince's anger has dissipated. They sing of Yin and Yang; the hanging paper moves in the wind when the percussionists play on its surface with drum sticks; the seemingly calm surface of the dialogue covers the intense excitement of the lovers' feelings. In lines that need little interpretation, the symbol of tea for lovemaking is clear:

         oolong, dark dragon, rises.
         squeezing the moli, jasmine flower, opens.
         *pressing the loonching, dragon well, overflows.**

The lovers arrive at the village of Luyu. Silence alternates with the wind in the rustling paper and then the sound builds in throbbing rhythms played on ceramic pots and stones, suggesting the inevitability of what is to come. The chorus becomes the voice of the elements. Luyu's daughter, Lu, offers a ritual tea ceremony for Lan and Seikyo. Together they taste the tea. She explains that her father has died. She knows why they have come: word of the wager between

---

*Oolong, Moli and Loonching are famous kinds of China tea.

Seikyo and the Prince has preceded them. She intones, "After this tea, home..." The ambitious Seikyo will not accept the world of tea, love, and meditation, his first thought is to keep *The Book of Tea* from the Prince. Lan is dismayed by his words. The agony of having to choose between her brother and her lover surfaces once more. In an aria filled with lyricism, Lu tells the couple that if the book binds their love together and if they promise to spread the word of the book to the world, then it is theirs. She hands it to Lan, who reads as Seikyo exults, "I have won." Lan angrily responds, "You win a book, I lose a brother!"

Suddenly the Prince appears and snatches the book from Lan's hands. The Prince laughs and quotes from *The Monkey King*: "Live or die, I shall never put down my sword until I get the true sutra [book] from paradise." The Prince and Seikyo fight, the desperate Lan tries to intervene by throwing herself between the two men. The Prince lunges at Seikyo but his sword finds its mark in his sister's breast. The dying Lan begs them not to weep for her.

Lu prepares a final tea ceremony as the Emperor arrives. Kneeling by his dying daughter, he mourns:

> *fare thee **well**,*
> ***well** til we meet in **dreams**,*
> ***dreams** in which we are spared the **pain**,*
> ***pain** which brings us endless **tears**,*
> ***tears** that rain, hard and **clear**.*
> ***clear** and loud as death **bells**,*
> ***bells** which toll **forever**,*
> ***forever** you and I play Monkey King.*

The Prince hands Seikyo his sword: "With me it began, with me it shall end." But, choosing not kill his foe, Seikyo cuts off his own long dark hair instead:

> *if water can forgive, if fire can stop worrying*
> *if wind can join us – after this tea, home...*

This deep sense of spiritual acceptance, expressed in the

repetition of Lan's last words, is underscored by cellos as the scene fades to black.

The brief final scene returns to the tea garden in Kyoto. Seikyo performs the tea ceremony, sipping from an empty cup. The monks intone:

> *though bowl is empty, scent glows,*
> *though shadow is gone, dream grows...*

while, to a haunting rhythm played on water, Seikyo ends the opera with the line:

> *savoring tea is the hardest...*
> *tea...*
> *a mirror of soul.*

The mystery of this work of opera theatre is not to be unraveled in these pages; the experience of *Tea* is highly personal between the individual sitting in the darkened space and all that happens on the stage. While recognizing this we do, on some inexplicable level, share Tan Dun's vision of love, nature, and of tea. *Tea* creates its own world of mystery and metaphor. The poetry in the lines of the libretto is pleasing on a visual as well as a perceptual level.

Chinese theatre has a long tradition of plays which present works with multiple levels of meaning. The opening line of the opera, "Tea: a mirror of soul," may refer to the Confucian concept of ritual as an outward form of an inward ethic. According to F. R. Carpenter, translator of Lu Yu's *Book of Tea*, "Tea was always a mirror of its cultural milieu even as it helped shape that culture." Thus, the outward actions of the characters in the ritual of the tea ceremony reflect not only their inner feelings, but also the ethics and traditions of ninth-century China. The setting of the tea ceremony as an allegory for the love story also celebrates the Taoist belief that every moment is special; every tea hour, just as every hour spent with the beloved, should be a masterpiece, to be lived as if it might never happen again. In teaching "Go with beauty, drink tea with beauty," the tea ceremony suggests

"Live with beauty."

Though the tea ceremony itself is performed in near-silence, allowing participants to be fully involved and present, an opera requires words that will be sung. In *Tea* both words and music are used sparingly and poetically to describe, in Tan Dun's words, the duality of "the spiritual inner space and its physical external counterpart."

The origins of tea are believed to go back to the third millennium BC in China. It was probably first used as a medicine, then as a food spice, before becoming a popular drink by the time of Confucius (551-479 BC). The botanical name for tea is *thea sinensis* or *camellia sinensis*. Thea (tea) was the name of the pre-Hellenic Titan goddess of light, of sight and of clear blue skies, the daughter of Uranus and Gaea; so tea is typically regarded as embodying the soft, gentle, yielding attributes of the feminine. Tea comes from a shrub that can grow to a height of 50 feet with a lifespan of 70 years, but in production the plant is kept pruned for the best leaves. The tea leaf is leathery, green, and shiny; its flower, the camellia, is white with yellow stamens. Much ritual and tradition goes into the picking, production, and making of tea. Tea has a calming, psychotropic effect that induces a mood of beauty and harmony in moderation. There is nothing rushed about the tea ceremony; the opera mirrors this in the slow, considered movements of the players, like a walking meditation.

The Chinese symbol for tea, "ch'a," first appeared in the fourth century A.D. Tea became a highly prized national drink from the seventh to tenth centuries, the time of the Tang Dynasty and the period in which the opera is set. In these years tea leaves were pounded into a solid brick or cake, part of which would be shaved off to make tea. Later, tea was produced in a powdered form from green tea leaves making a frothy drink; the Japanese to this day use such a tea, called *matcha*, in their tea ceremonies. By the 14th century tea was made from loose leaves, the way we enjoy it today.

The tea ceremony arrived in Japan from China when, the story goes, one Esai, a 12th-century Zen Buddhist monk, brought tea seeds back and cultivated them in his garden. Another story tells how the tea ceremony grew out of the custom of Buddhist monks drinking tea from a communal bowl, and their discovery that the stimulant in tea helped their meditation in terms of focus and clarity. From these beginnings the *Cha No Yu*, or the Japanese tea ceremony, evolved. The great Tea Master Rikyu began the tradition of the tea ceremony in the late 16th century, a tradition which has been passed down from generation to generation to the present day. The two ceremonies, Chinese and Japanese, are quite different: the Chinese focus on the tea itself and on tea drinking, while the Japanese *Cha No Yu* is more formalized, focusing on the ritualistic and Zen aspects of the ceremony.

The tea ceremony rests on four principles: harmony with people and nature, respect for others, purity of heart and mind, and tranquillity. The ceremonies combine many Eastern philosophies: the bitter taste of tea can refer to Buddhist suffering; in Confucianism the tea ceremony teaches harmony and balance; in Taoism tea represents the essence of nature, believing that every act of living is important and beauty may be found everywhere in the world. The ritual of tea recognizes that the mundane and the particular are as important as the spiritual and universal. The formalized acts of politeness in the tea ceremony are the outward expressions of an inner belief in the value of peace and harmony – thus the opera's subtitle, "Mirror of Soul."

Tea took on great cultural significance in China and Japan when an extraordinary treatise, *Ch'a Ching*, or *The Book of Tea*, was written by the eighth-century Chinese scholar Lu Yu. This is the same *Book of Tea* that is so central to the opera. Elevating the preparation and drinking of tea to a spiritual ritual, Lu Yu described the atmosphere in which the tea should be enjoyed and the appropriate state of mind of the participant, as well as designing the very specific implements for the ceremony.

Statue of Lu Yu
Jiangxi Provence, China

Known as the Sage of Tea, or the patron saint of tea, Lu Yu was raised by Buddhist monks in China. Unwilling to become a monk himself, he left the monastery in his early teens and set out on his own. After many years of adventures and travels, he settled down in the mountainous region of

Zhejiang Province in southern China to write *Ch'a Ching* over a period of five years, completing it in 780 A.D. He described the growing, picking, and manufacture of tea, the best water to use, and how tea should be sipped slowly in order to savor the flavor. He related tea drinking to a right way of living, finding in the tea ceremony the same harmony and order that rules all other aspects of life. In the *Ch'a Ching* he wrote:

> *The best quality of tea must have the creases like the*
> *leather boots of Tartar horsemen,*
> *Curl like the dewlap of a mighty bullock, unfold like a*
> *mist rising out of a ravine,*
> *Gleam like a lake touched by a zephyr, and be wet and*
> *soft like earth newly swept by rain.*

Much of Tan Dun's opera is based on Lu Yu's *Book of Tea*. The entire libretto, at the simplest level, re-enacts the tea ceremony while, in performance, the opera suggests many deeper levels of meaning. The act of drinking tea may indeed be likened to an act of love since it encompasses all the attributes of love: harmony, respect, the enjoyment of all that is beautiful, of nature and beauty and the senses of touch, smell, sight, taste and sound. The ethereal quality of tea can haunt us and be remembered just as a tender love relationship may be remembered many years after it has ended. The opera touches all these aspects. The composer describes Lan, the mistress of tea, as a metaphor for love.

How Tan Dun came to compose an opera encompassing both Chinese and Western styles of music is a story worthy of an opera itself. Born in 1957 in a village in central Hunan, a south western province of China, Tan Dun was raised as a young child by his grandmother until his family fell victim of the dictates of Mao Tse Tung who, in Mao's Cultural Revolution (1965-1975), decreed that all intellectuals had to be sent away from their homes to be "re-educated" by the peasants. Accordingly, in the mid 1970s, the teenaged Tan

Dun was sent away to a commune where he spent two years working alongside the peasants planting rice and tending pigs. While at the commune he collected folk songs from his neighbors and soon led the village's musical celebrations for local events.

Fate then stepped in when a boat carrying a visiting Peking Opera troupe capsized in a nearby river and some of the musicians drowned. Needing replacements, Tan Dun was recruited and, for the next couple of years, he traveled and played with the Peking Opera, becoming immersed in this ancient art form. At this time the Peking Opera was only allowed to present plays that promoted Mao's dogma. In *The Eight Model Plays* all references to the aristocratic or old way of life were deleted. The Peking Opera was used as a tool with which to educate the masses in the teachings of Mao. These must have been conflicting years for the young Tan Dun, who had been raised with the ancient shamanic traditions of southern China and the animistic idea that spirits exist in everything everywhere – in the trees, the wind, stones – and that the entire universe has a life and soul.

After the Cultural Revolution, the Central Conservatory of Music in Beijing re-opened and was overwhelmed with thousands of students seeking admission. Tan Dun, who had never heard Mozart or Beethoven (both were banned by Mao), did have experience as a musician from the Peking Opera and knew 500 folk songs from the country; he was accepted. For the next eight years, in addition to studying Chinese musical forms, Tan Dun was exposed to the vast repertoire of Western music. His compositions began to incorporate Western serialism alongside traditional Chinese music. Influenced by visiting composers such as Takemitsu, Crumb and Henze, Tan Dun led the "New Wave" in controversial music in Asia, meeting with disapproval from many critics and praise from others.

Tan Dun also pioneered the re-discovery of music from China's ancient past. At 22, he composed his first symphony, *Li Sao*, a poetic lament based on fourth-century traditions from his own Hunan province. His orchestral work *On Taoism* (1985) was a turning point. Blending Chinese and Western music with extraordinary originality, this composition placed Tan Dun firmly on the international map.

In 1986 he was offered a fellowship at Columbia University by Professor Chou Wen-chung who was then Vice Dean for Academic Affairs and chairman of the Music Division at the School of the Arts. Tan Dun moved to New York, where he found himself lost in a tidal wave of new music and experiences. It took a little while for him to regain his balance and compose again. He drew, he said, "on Chinese colors, on the techniques of the Peking Opera, and began to find a way to mingle old materials from my culture with the new, to contribute something to the western idea of atonality and to refresh it." His new compositions included "organic" instruments that spring from nature, such as the 50 ceramic pots he used in *Nine Songs* (1989). In the 1990s Tan Dun pursued many different paths and by the end of the century his music, both as a conductor and a composer, became truly global both in spirit and in concept.

In his opera *Marco Polo* (1996), Tan Dun sought to develop a 21st-century opera that incorporated multiple languages, cultures, and time periods. Marco Polo's famous 13th-century journey became a symbol for journeying on many levels. The opera, *Peony Pavilion*, (1998) recreates a masterpiece of the 16th century, evoking the Ming Dynasty's Chinese theatre with multi electronic and digital effects. Tan Dun also composed the score for the soundtrack of the movie *Crouching Tiger, Hidden Dragon*, for which he was awarded both an Oscar and a Grammy. In December 2006 his opera *The First Emperor* premiered at the Metropolitan

Opera, New York.

For Tan Dun, the most important elements in writing music are "balance and counterpoint," not just in style and tempo but in a much broader sense as well. He sees no boundaries between set design and instruments, between musicians and singers, between the instruments of a conventional orchestra and "organic" music using paper, water, and ceramic pots, between audience and performers. The three female percussionists on stage in *Tea* represent the spirits of rebirth (water), wind (paper), and fate (earthenware and stones). At different points the musicians flip the pages of their scores back and forth loudly and in unison to recreate the sound of wind and rustling trees.

Tan Dun has said, "Music is the wellspring of internal feelings, and my music is completely based on the Chinese culture." *Tea* however incorporates both the Japanese as well as the Chinese tea ceremony, endowing both with a similar sense of spiritual and sensual power. In researching *Tea*, Tan Dun traveled extensively in China and Japan studying tea ceremonies. He was most impressed by a nun in southern China who always presents her guests with an empty tea bowl, and then puts the empty bowl to her lips, as if to drain it. "For me," Tan Dun said, "there was something greatly enlightening about the spirit of Chinese tea as made manifest in her." The enigma of drinking tea from an empty bowl is captured in these words from the *I Ching* which says: "Only by virtue of its emptiness can it receive." The gesture of drinking from the empty tea bowl, which opens and closes Tan Dun's opera, suggests the need to remain open to all that is, in a state of tranquil acceptance.

Tea: A Mirror of Soul was co-commissioned by Suntory Hall, Tokyo, the Shanghai Grand Theatre and the Netherlands Opera. The premiere was held at Suntory Hall in October, 2002. Further performances were presented in Amsterdam in 2003, in Lyon, France (2004) and Wellington,

New Zealand (2006). All met with critical acclaim. The presentation of *Tea* at The Santa Fe Opera in the summer of 2007 marks its American premiere.

Tea creates its own mystical world. Tan Dun may be a collector of folk songs, a spiritual mathematician (his own words), and a composer, but more than these he is, perhaps, a true shaman, with music the means of his magical power.

Characters		**Metaphor for:**
Lan, Chinese Princess	Soprano	Love
Seikyo, Prince and		
Japanese monk	Baritone	Discovery/philosophy
The Prince, Lan's brother	Tenor	Anger
The Emperor, father of		
Lan and the Prince	Bass	Tradition/culture
Lu, Luyu's daughter,		
and Ritualist	Contralto	Tea/spirit messenger
Monks	Bass baritones	Religion
Orchestra		Drama
3 percussionists play water, paper,		
and ceramic instruments		Nature

Bibliography

Lu Yu. *The Classic of Tea*, Francis Ross Carpenter, trans. Little Brown & Co. (Canada) 1974

Manchester, Carole, *Tea in the East*. William Morrow and Co. Inc., 1996.

Sen Genshitsu, *The Enjoyment of Tea*, Tankosha Publishing Co. Ltd., Japan, 2006

Tan Dun: *Biography in Depth*. www.tandunonline.com.

Tan Dun, *Tea: A Mirror of Soul*, libretto. G. Schirmer, Inc., New York, 2002.

Tan Dun, *Tea: A Mirror of Soul*, Deutsche Grammophon DVD,
B0003851-09, 2002.

Tokyo Journal, "Varied and Profound, the pleasure of creative
observation directly touches the essence of life itself." Japan,
November 2, 2002

Personal communication, Tan Dun, composer and
Peggy Monastra, Director of Promotion, G. Schirmer Inc.,
New York, February 2007.

Personal communication, Frank Murphy, lecturer and
connoisseur of China tea, Santa Fe, NM, December 2006

Personal communication, Megan Hill, student in the Urasenke
Japanese Tea Ceremony tradition, Santa Fe, December 2006

Daphne

Richard Strauss

"**G**olden is Apollo's tunic and golden his mantle, his bow and his quiver. No one has his skill. He is the archer, the minstrel, and he keeps those arts alive." Thus goes the ancient Greek Hymn to Apollo, the god who fell in love with and pursued the earthly nymph, Daphne. The myth of Daphne and Apollo has long been a favorite of artists and composers. Richard Strauss was drawn to the subject when he saw Bernini's statue of the transformation of Daphne in the Villa Borghese in Rome. (The statue appears on the cover of this book.)

Strauss was attracted to myth as subject matter throughout his long career. *Ariadne auf Naxos* (1916) and *Die Äegyptische Helena* (1928) were both treated in a humorous vein, but not so *Daphne*, to which he turned in 1935. *Daphne*, with no humor or sub plots, is a romantic tone poem subtitled "A Bucolic Tragedy in one act." Strauss composed this opera, a paean to nature, at his lovely home in Garmisch, high in the Bavarian Alps, at a time when Europe was racing headlong towards a catastrophic world war. Choosing not to compose *Daphne* in the style of the early 20th century, Strauss looked back instead to a post-romantic style that paid homage to Hellenic classicism. By the time of *Daphne*, the 13th of his 15 operas, the 71-year-old Strauss was well established and independent, a law unto himself.

His collaboration on the opera with Joseph Gregor, the librettist, extended over a three-year period, during which time Gregor conferred with Strauss at his home in Garmisch many times to discuss the ongoing work. The libretto grew from three different versions that Gregor prepared. The conductor Karl Böhm, to whom the opera was dedicated, recalled that, on one visit to Garmisch, he observed Gregor writing the libretto upstairs, while Strauss, downstairs, set the pages to music. Strauss completed the score in Sicily on Christmas Eve 1937 and the premiere was given in October 1938 at the Dresden Staatsoper, scene of so many of Strauss's first nights. The opera, paired with Strauss's *Friedenstag*, was well received and soon appeared at opera houses all over Germany, in spite of the deteriorating political situation. John Crosby, founder of The Santa Fe Opera, was the first person to bring *Daphne* to America with a Santa Fe production in 1964.

The music is melodic and flowing, a lyrical poem which tells the tale with much passion and psychological insight. Delicate and transparent at times, the score is solemn and dramatic at others. It is most compelling in its depiction of the rustic atmosphere of the world of nature, for this truly is a nature tale: Daphne, part child, part nymph, is in love with the beauty of nature that she finds all around her in the trees, the flowers, and the sunlight. She sings her opening aria, "O bleib, geliebter Tag" (O stay, beloved day), to her brothers the trees and her sisters the flowers. In love with the day and the sun's light, she fears the cold, dark night, and is unsettled by the imminent feast of Dionysus: "The clumsy people trampling the grass, their savage singing offends my ear!" She longs for the shelter the trees provide after Apollo, the mighty god of the sun, completes his ride across the heavens and enters Mt. Olympus at the close of the day. The enraptured Daphne embraces the tree to music that is sweet and mysterious, in a mood of delicate impressionism.

Daphne is the daughter of Peneios, a onetime river god and now a fisherman married to Gaea, the Earth Mother. So Daphne is thus of the river and the earth, as well as a follower of Artemis, the virgin huntress who was Apollo's twin. The opera's setting, by the side of the river named after Peneios, is in view of Mount Olympus, home of the gods. Peneios's humble dwelling stands by the riverside. It is dusk, time of the setting sun on Midsummer's Eve on the feast of Dionysus, a time of revelry and mating when the annual fertility rites are observed. Cattle and sheep can be heard in the distance, and in the score, where an alphorn sounds above the orchestra depicting the rustic scene. (When alphorns are not available, trombones are generally substituted.) The shepherds come in from the fields, anticipating the festivities of the night. They place "garlands in [their] hair and anoint [their] limbs to honor the god of wine," as the sun fades and night approaches.

The childlike Daphne enters alone and sings of her love of nature and the trees. She is startled at the end of her song when Leukippos, her childhood friend, jumps out from behind a tree. Leukippos loves the young girl and would speak to her of love. He reminds her of how she was charmed by the music of his flute. Daphne tells him she heard in his music "the swelling of the wind kissing the blossoms." Leukippos longs for her, but she always runs from him, "resembling in [her] flight the goddess Diana." Now, Leukippos tells her, on the feast of Dionysus he is a man with a man's yearning and will play no more. With this he breaks his flute and attempts to embrace Daphne. She struggles free, and Leukippos sadly leaves.

Daphne's mother, Gaea, has observed her daughter's rejection of the young man and tells her, "The will of the gods demands that you open your heart like a blossom and turn to love." But Daphne is not ready. Two maids enter with a beautiful dress and jewelry for her to wear at the feast, but she sends them away, choosing to remain in her simple clothes. A concerned Gaea leads her daughter into the house.

The maids wonder why Daphne will not wear the lovely dress then, spotting the sorrowful Leukippos, they call to him. They tell him they are magical beings and suggest that he wear Daphne's clothes so that, disguised as a woman, he can be near her at the feast. At first Leukippos declines, but eventually he goes along with the plan.

Peneios now enters and stands awed by "the shimmering crimson cloud around the summit of Olympus's peak." Once a god himself, he invites the gods of Olympus to return to the hut of their former brother for the feast. (We are not told why Peneios is no longer a god.) Gaea, his wife, chides him for aspiring to such heights. Peneios insists they must prepare, for he sees the gods approaching in the distance, attracted by the smell of roasting meat and the aroma of wine. Phoebus Apollo, he says, is amongst them. Gaea warns: "Do not challenge the gods, joy lies in being one with the earth." Neither realizes that Apollo does indeed attend the feast, but in the guise of a cowherd and with an ulterior motive – not to honor Dionysus or Peneios, but to pursue Daphne, the daughter of Peneios.

Suddenly there is a flash of red lightning and Apollo enters, dressed as a simple cowherd and carrying a bow and arrows. He greets Peneios and Gaea and explains that his cattle stampeded and galloped to the river at the smell of the feast. Peneios orders that Daphne be sent for so that she may serve their guest. The moon rises as Daphne appears carrying a goblet and a cloak. She offers the cup to the stranger, who is overcome by her beauty. Believing Daphne to be his beloved sister, Artemis, he addresses her as: "Sister," a name to which she happily responds. He kneels as Daphne removes his bow and arrows. When she places the blue mantle on his shoulders, a strange radiance emanates from it. She wonders who this "miraculous stranger, mighty shepherd" is. He tells her that when he saw her from the heavens his chariot halted at the sight of her beauty. He quotes Daphne's own words about never wanting the day to end. She, trusting him as a brother, sinks into his arms; and he enfolds her in his mantle and kisses her passionately. Expecting a brotherly kiss, Daphne suddenly understands what is happening and struggles free of the god's embrace. (One finds reference here to Wagner and Parsifal's enlightenment on being kissed by a "motherly" Kundry.) Daphne feels betrayed; the stranger came by stealth and tried to hold her against her will. Apollo begs her to waken to his love, but she will have none of him.

A procession of shepherds and revelers now enters, with Peneios at their head. Daphne runs to her mother and the women, Apollo joins the men. Paying homage to Dionysus, the men and women intermingle while masked men perform a wild dance as "rams" with the "baccantes," the female followers of Bacchus. A group of Daphne's girlfriends approaches, one of whom, (Leukippos in disguise), offers her a drink and asks her to dance. They move together in a slow dance until the jealous cowherd, Apollo, cries out that this is blasphemy. The shepherds are insulted and demand to know why the stranger disrupts their feast. They threaten him and tear off his mantle. The infuriated god loses his temper and fires an arrow into the sky, causing mighty rumbles of thunder. The frightened shepherds run off to tend their flocks, leaving Apollo, Daphne, and Leukippos alone.

Apollo denounces Leukippos, who throws off his woman's dress and admits his deception. Daphne now feels doubly deceived, first by the stranger, now by Leukippos. Daphne and Leukippos demand that the stranger tell them who he is. Defiantly and triumphantly, he responds: "Every jubilant morning I grasp the bridle and mount the magnificent chariot." He is the god of the sun. Daphne realizes that in her heart she sensed this, while Leukippos calls him a liar and curses him. This is too much for Apollo, who raises his bow and shoots. Lightning flashes in the sky and Leukippos falls. Daphne runs to his side and sings to her dying friend. Now, too late, she understands Leukippos's love, and, again, too late, she is ready to respond. She ends her long, exquisite aria with the promise that she will stay by Leukippos's graveside until death also comes for her.

The watching, guilty Apollo now reverts to his godlike self and sings a magnificent aria, "Gotter! Bruder im hohen Olympus" (Gods! Brothers in high Olympus), with all the power of a youthful, heroic tenor voice. He asks himself, "Am I a god still – or diminished and humbled by human emotion?" He begs Dionysus for forgiveness for having desecrated his feast and for slaying Leukippos, who sang his praises. He asks Zeus to: "Fulfill her desire, all her longing! Let her reach among her companions, the trees in blossom, towards our domain." Then he sings his famous decree: "This evergreen branch, sister, shall be a symbol worn by heroes as a crown. You will gently encircle the foreheads of the bravest of mortals, rewarding their valor, ennobling forever the heroes of mankind." With this, he disappears into the black night. Daphne runs upstage, then suddenly stands still, singing, "The earth is in me! Let me greet you, life-giving light! Apollo! Brother! Make me a symbol of love never-ending." As she is slowly transformed into the laurel tree, her words become sounds emanating from the branches, as she is consumed by the ecstatic music of transformation in what Alex Ross calls an "atmosphere of untouchable serenity."

The extraordinary ending of this opera, is one of the most magical passages in all of Strauss's music, and one of the most theatrically affecting. Strauss had resisted Gregor's suggestion that Peneios, Gaea, and the shepherds return after the transformation to sing a choral hymn of thanksgiving.

The composer stood firm: "Away with all distractions – the tree alone will sing!"

The major source of the opera comes from Ovid's book, *Metamorphoses*, written in the first century AD. Originally the tale was told to provide an account of the origin of the laurel tree – Daphne means laurel in Greek – and how its leaves came to wreath and encircle the brows of heroes. The story of the pursuit of Daphne by Apollo was a means to an end, told in a mock-heroic style; Ovid delighted in parodying the great god. For Apollo, it appears, was not always the glorious sun god who rode across the heavens bringing light. He was typically unlucky in love, rejected more than once by the women, nymphs, and goddesses he pursued. Though he is the patron god of healing, poetry, music, and archery, and an unerring prophet and diviner, with Daphne all his godlike attributes appear to desert him. Ovid makes him look like a fool.

Ovid's literary treatment of the myth is written as a poetic fiction that begins with Cupid (who does not appear in the opera) as the instigator of the plot. Cupid is stringing his small bow one day when Apollo scolds him: "Silly youngster, what are you doing with such weapons? These are for grown-ups! The bow is for my shoulders. The torch is enough for you to play with to get the love-fires burning. Do not meddle with honors that are mine." The insulted Cupid replies, "My bow will fix you." He fires a golden arrow into Apollo, who falls in love at once with the earthly nymph Daphne. Cupid then fires a lead-tipped arrow into Daphne to ensure that she will never return Apollo's love.

The firing of Cupid's two arrows jump-starts the action. Apollo, having put away his sun chariot for the night, descends from the heavens, disguises himself as a cowherd, and comes to the feast of Dionysus seeking Daphne, his first love. He cannot imagine that she will not have him and is somewhat taken aback when Daphne, an innocent child of nature, runs from his embrace. In the ludicrous chase that follows he woos her on the run, telling her he is: "Lord of Delphi, Jove is my father. The power of healing is my discovery." The juxtaposition of the god's noble words with his ineffectual chase of the girl is pure farce and reaches a further low level when Ovid compares the god to a hound chasing a terrified hare.

Apollo has almost caught up with Daphne when she cries to the river of her father, "If there is any power in the river, change and destroy the body which has given too much delight." No sooner said than done: "Her limbs grew heavy, her soft breasts were enclosed in soft bark, her hair became leaves, her arms branches, her speedy feet rooted and held, her head became a tree top. Everything gone, except her grace, her shining." Apollo is left hugging a tree. "He placed his hand [on the tree] and felt the heart still beating under the bark." He then announces, "'Let the laurel adorn, henceforth, my hair, my lyre, my quiver. Let Roman victors wear laurel wreaths for triumph and ovation. Let the laurel always be green and shining.' The laurel, stirring, seemed to consent, to be saying *Yes.*" There is irony in the fact that the laurel wreath, intended as a symbol of victory, becomes, for Apollo, a symbol of defeat in love, while for Daphne the laurel represents a symbol of purity and the crown which, in later religious symbology, virgins attain in heaven for an exemplary life on earth.

This is the genesis of the myth, which itself has undergone many transformations since Ovid first described it at the beginning of the Christian era. In the Middle Ages Apollo was depicted as a courtly lover burdened with sorrow at the inaccessibility of his lady. Petrarch, in the early 14th century, cast Daphne as the unattainable courtly lady and Apollo as her poet-lover who must forever adore her from a distance. Ovid's tale later became an allegory of moral wisdom in which the two poles of Christian duality, those of divine and sensual love, were interpreted. The Christianization of the myth included depicting Apollo as both Satan, persecuting the human soul, and Christ, attempting union with sinful humanity. Daphne stood then for the Christian soul and the laurel for the true cross! In medieval Christian terms, the story symbolizes the battle between the flesh and the spirit. By the time of Richard Strauss in the 20th-century, it is the romantic genre that sets the tone for the tale.

Metamorphosis is an intriguing concept. This "change of form" occurs most obviously in nature: tadpoles turn into frogs, chrysalises into butterflies, and so forth. Nature provided the model for myth and literature. The Greek gods were constantly transforming themselves, their victims, and the objects of their desire into mortals, animals, and plants at will.

Transformation was often punitive, as when Arachne was turned into a spider after she defied Minerva; Circe turned Odysseus's men into pigs when they trespassed on her island; Acteon was turned into a stag by Artemis for inadvertently having seen her bathe naked, and Callisto was turned into a bear by Zeus's jealous wife, Hera. Zeus frequently turned himself into another form to pursue women, appearing to Europa as a bull, to Leda as a swan, to Danae as a shower of gold. (Danae's story became the focus of Richard Strauss's next opera, *Die Liebe der Danae*.) Hoping to hide his indiscretion from his wife, Zeus turned Io into a white heifer – to no avail, for Hera then persecuted Io, the heifer, by sending a gadfly to torment her, chasing her all over the world. Sometimes, however, there was a positive outcome, such as when Pygmalion fell in love with a statue he had made and Venus took pity on him and transformed the stone into a living woman. Apollo frequently changed shape, becoming a cowherd in *Daphne*, a crow and an old woman at other times. At one point, Ovid reports, when escaping some menace, all the gods changed shape: "Jove was a ram, Apollo hid as a crow, his sister was a cat, Bacchus a goat, Juno a snow-white heifer, Venus a fish, Mercury a flamingo."

Celtic myths also contain many transformations: Aoife changes her stepchildren into swans to be rid of them, and the wife of Finn MacCumaill is changed into a deer by a druidic priest. Fairies, witches, wizards, and shamans all have shape-shifting abilities. Merlin changed Arthur into various animals in order that he might learn from them. In Wagner's mythic *Ring* cycle, derived from Nordic sagas, transformations occur with the help of the tarnhelm, a magic helmet: Alberich the dwarf becomes a toad, a giant becomes a dragon, Siegfried becomes his host Günther.

Metamorphosis, or shape-shifting as it is also called, exists in the mythological stories of most lands. Transformation stories about werewolves and Dr. Jekyll and Mr. Hyde provide fodder for horror movies today, while the Frog Prince is the stuff of fairy tales, reminding us that shape-changing can be for both good and evil.

In contemporary literature, the *Metamorphosis* of Franz Kafka springs to mind, an almost unbearable tale of an ordinary traveling salesman who turns into a large beetle overnight, of his family who persecute him and ultimately cause his death. In *Finnegans Wake*, James Joyce writes of two gossiping washerwomen on either side of the river Liffey who are turned into an elm and a stone: "Are you not gone ahome?... My foos wont moos. I feel as old as yonder elm... Night! Night! I feel as heavy as yonder stone. Tell me, elm! Telmetale of stem or stone. Beside the rivering waters of... Night!"

The aging Richard Strauss composed one further work, the *Metamorphosen* for 23 solo strings, on this subject that so clearly appealed to him. Written in 1945 during the last days of a terrible war that had all but destroyed Strauss's beloved opera houses at Dresden and Munich, the work was a lament for all that had been lost. "The world's most holy shrines – destroyed," he wrote to Joseph Gregor at the time.

For many, metamorphosis was a punishment, one that was rarely reversed. For Daphne, however, it was a means of escape and liberation, a way of worshiping the god forever as a tree, opening to the sun, and being one with her brothers and sisters in nature. For Daphne, in love with nature and the life-giving light of Apollo, her deepest desire was fulfilled. Strauss glorifies her metamorphosis in music that combines his musical nature poetry with the themes of Apollo and the pastoral theme of Daphne herself in music that literally shimmers, leaving, in the end, the transformed Daphne standing alone on the stage as a laurel tree, drenched in moonlight, awaiting the return of day.

Characters

Peneios	bass
Gaea	contralto
Daphne	soprano
Leukippos	tenor
Apollo	tenor

Bibliography

Barnard, Mary E. *The Myth of Apollo and Daphne*. Duke University Press, 1987.

Gregor, Joseph. *Daphne*, libretto. Maria Pelikan, trans., Boosey & Hawkes Music Publishers Inc., 1965.

Joyce, James. *Finnegans Wake*. New York: Viking Press, 1967.

Ovid. *Metamorphoses*. Rolfe Humphries, trans., Indiana University Press, 1955.

Ross, Alex. "The Last Emperor: Richard Strauss." *The New Yorker*, Dec. 20, 1999.

L'Homme Grenouille (The Frog Man)
after Nicolo dell' Abbate

Platée

Jean-Phillipe Rameau

*W*hen the gods are bored, mere mortals had better watch out! Dire consequences usually result when bored gods meddle in human affairs for their own amusement. In the case of *Platée*, the victim is a marsh nymph, who is more marsh than nymph, and who is generally portrayed as a frog-like creature, complete with croaking sounds: *"Quoi, quoi!"* She is used by the great god, Jupiter, for his own ends. After raising her hopes to high heaven, the laughing god cruelly drops her back into the marsh when he is done with her. This opera, in the style of late French Baroque, is called both a *ballet bouffon*, since there are as many dance sequences as sung ones, and a *comédie lyrique*, indicating that there is singing as well. Depending on one's sense of humor, *Platée* may also be called a cruel practical joke.

Platée was written by Jean-Philippe Rameau (1683 - 1764). The most successful French composer of his time, he rose to his particular niche of fame in the mid-18th century, tucked in between the highly respected composers Jean-Baptiste Lully (1632 - 87) and Christoph Gluck (1714 - 87). In these early years of opera, the French preferred a classical, declamatory style and were dismayed by the liberties taken with operatic form by the Italians across their border. Prior to the Revolution, French opera was quite different to our experience today. Royalty and the nobility, the primary patrons of opera and ballet, commissioned and paid for everything, building theatres that often seated more than 1,000 people in their palaces, gardens, and great houses, and footing the bill for wildly extravagant spectacles. In the years when Rameau was composing, the performances at Versailles were legendary.

In 1672, Louis XIVth gave Lully, the leading composer of the day and a favorite at court, a monopoly on public performances of opera and ballet at the Académie Royale de Musique – the early incarnation of the Paris Opéra, or Opéra Garnier as we know it today. Located in the Palais Royale, this formidable theatre held 1,270 people, about half of whom stood in the parterre. An evening's entertainment consisted of ballet, spectacle, and opera, with opera the least important of the three.

The French were proud of their great classical tradition and their magnificent tragic dramas, which extolled the French language. They preferred to keep their drama quite separate from their ballet and music. To a certain extent Lully managed to combine classical tragedy, the pastorale, Italian opera, and French ballet, while cutting all comic scenes during his time at the Académie. In so doing, he laid the groundwork for a French national opera that was to last for 100 years. His operas paid homage to the king and were written with the French court in mind at all times. It was said of Lully that he combined "musical talent, ruthlessness, commercial shrewdness, and obsequious manners" to achieve success at both the court and the Académie. Designed to please the eye and the ear, his works contained little action or passion, and no humor; in his plots, the greater emphasis was on spectacular staging and, of course, the ballet.

Following Lully's death in 1687, a struggle emerged between the supporters of French and Italian styles of opera.

The newly arrived Rameau had to defend himself from attack following the debut of his very first opera, *Hippolyte et Aricie*, in 1733. The old guard, the "Lullistes," really took exception to the "Ramistes," the avant-garde followers of Rameau, who supported the success of his early operas.

Rameau was already 40 years old when he arrived in Paris. He traveled to the French capital to promote his theoretical book, *Traité de l'Harmonie*, the first of his long series of books on music theory and harmony, some of which are still in use today. He had been a church organist, teacher and composer of harpsichord music. Now, in Paris, he wanted to compose operas. His first opera, a *tragédie-lyrique*, was presented at the Académie when the composer was 50. Over the next 12 years Rameau produced works that were either *tragédie en musique* or *opéra-ballets*. All met with success, and he was hailed as the new Orpheus of French opera.

Platée premiered at the court of Versailles in 1745. Jean-Jacques Rousseau called the opera "M. Rameau's masterpiece and the most excellent piece of music that has been heard up to now in our theatres." This was before the eruption of the Querelle des Bouffons (War of the Buffoons), a war about music styles that was fought out in letters and pamphlets, the 18th-century equivalent of our media, over a period of two years from 1752 to 54. The battle was sparked by performances of an Italian troupe, called *Bouffons*, at the Académie. Diderot, Rousseau, and Baron Grimm led those who hailed Italian opera as the style of the future, while Rameau and his followers were attacked for composing operas that continued to emphasize the dramatic elements of French style while introducing advanced harmonic and orchestral writing. French opera had become staid, it was claimed, although Lully, the old master, was still revered. Rameau, while well established, was still not widely accepted as the standard-bearer of a new and improved French style. There was an impasse, with most of Paris taking one side or the other in the debate.

The root cause for this "war" lay deeper, however, than the issue of the relative superiority of French or Italian opera. Louis XVth had handed over the management of the Académie to the City of Paris, thus lightening the royal purse (even for Louis, the upkeep of a big theatre was a major burden). Without royal patronage, the theatre found itself struggling. Tired of Lully and the old style, audiences were ready for something new to revitalize their opera. This was also the time of the rise of a cultured middle class who wanted to determine what was performed in the public theatres, independent of the king and court. To this end music theatres, called academies, were formed, and even coffee houses put on musical entertainments. Opera was moving out of palaces and great houses and into theatres with audiences who sought new music, new ideas, and new productions.

In the larger historical arena, the French court was already in decline, and royal absolutism was being challenged by Diderot, Rousseau, and other members of the Enlightenment. The shift of the public's allegiance from French to Italian opera was seen by the *ancien régime* as an act of disloyalty to the crown. Ultimately the new, fresh, forward-moving style of Italian opera won out over the traditional, more structured French style. In fact there should have been no argument, since the two styles are quite different and do not conflict with one another. As Grove points out, the French style was "noble, elevated and tragic," and the Italian, "light, farcical and comic;" they could easily have co-existed side by side. As it turned out, the two styles were forerunners of the *opera seria* and *opera buffa*, tragic and comic forms, which followed them. Rameau was caught in the middle of all these politics. Ironically, having first been criticized as pro-Italian in the Lullistes/Ramistes controversy, he later came under fire as part of the Establishment on the French side in the Querelle des Bouffons.

In *Platée*, Rameau clearly leans towards comedy, taking as his model the vaudeville and burlesque conventions of Paris's Fair or *Foire* theatres, most of which had been in existence since the Middle Ages. These theatres presented popular entertainments, farces, burlesques, and acrobatic displays. They parodied the opera of the court and evolved eventually into the peculiarly French style we know as *opéra-comique*. *Platée* satirizes the traditional form of opera for its extravagance, its spectacle, its language, and its adherence to the strict musical style inherited from Lully.

The premiere of *Platée* celebrated the occasion of the French Dauphin's wedding to the Spanish princess, Maria Teresa. It was said that Maria Teresa was a particularly unattractive woman and it was feared that Platée, the ugly frog who attempts to marry Jupiter, might be seen as a parody of the royal couple whom Rameau was supposed to honor. The coincidence passed unobserved, however, and nobody expressed any surprise or outrage at this new production in terms of either its content or style. A few months after the wedding, in fact, Rameau was offered two royal pensions and the title of Composer in the King's Chamber of Music, thus ensuring his future at court, where indeed he spent most of the remainder of his life.

Four years after the Versailles premiere, *Platée* was presented again at the Académie Royale de Musique, thus exposing the work to a wide public audience. In spite of its unconventionality, (or perhaps because of it), *Platée* was a success with both the court and the public and became part of the Académie's repertoire for the next 30 years. Then it simply disappeared until the 20th century, when it was revived and recognized as a superb example of the late French Baroque style in its most comic form.

The characters in *Platée* are a pot pourri of gods who live on Mount Olympus, and a bevy of marshy frog creatures

– already the gods are being parodied. Platée's situation would be truly tragic were it not for the fact that Rameau casts Platée, not as a vulnerable woman and a soprano, but as a high tenor (*haute-contre*), in drag, in what is known as a *travesti* role.

The opera commences with the obligatory Prologue, here called The Birth of Comedy. The long, foot-tapping overture accomplishes something quite new for Rameau's time: it closely connects the music with the drama to follow, introducing some of the melodies that will be heard later in the opera. Rameau set the work in a vineyard on the slopes of Mt. Cithéron in Greece. Contemporary productions tend to set the action in indeterminate places and times; since the essence of the story is timeless, setting it as the composer desired is not so vital.

Regardless of where the opera takes place, the Prologue opens on a scene of partying, dancing, and wine drinking. Thespis, the inventor of comedy, is discovered asleep on the stage, and the chorus wakes him up. Momus, the god of ridicule, and Thalia, the muse of comedy, arrive and plan with Thespis to present a play that will "correct the shortcomings of mortals" and address the manners of the gods whose "good behavior is oft times absent." Momus defends the gods: "Who could resist the boredom of being immortal and forever well-behaved?" Recalling that Jupiter once devised a plan to cure his wife, Juno, of jealousy and pride, he suggests that Thespis use Jupiter's ploy as the basis for his play. L'Amour (Eros) appears slightly miffed because she has not been consulted – how could there be a play without the inspiration of love, she asks. The plan is set in action as the chorus performs a *contredanse* in anticipation of a new entertainment.

So the stage is set for the play within a play. Act I begins with a storm in the orchestra out of which Mercury, Jupiter's messenger, descends from the heavens. He tells King

Cithéron that Jupiter is impatient with his wife's behavior, her uncontrollable jealousy and the raging storms she is creating to give vent to her anger. Mercury has been instructed to find some diversion for the god. Cithéron suggests that Jupiter might appear to be planning a new marriage with Platée, an ugly, but vain, creature from the marsh. Juno's jealousy will be defused when she sees Platée, she will forgive her husband and they will be reunited. Mercury thinks this will be great fun, an amusement for the entire heavenly court. Cithéron describes Platée to Mercury before he returns to heaven to tell Jupiter of their plan:

> *This laughable Naiad from all time proscribed by Love,*
> *Blindly unaware of her comic features,*
> *Hopes each day that a thousand lovers will come*
> > *in turn to worship her.*

The frog-like Platée now enters, a tenor in woman's clothes, and asks Cithéron why he does not express the love she is sure he feels for her. (One wonders if Cithéron did not propose Platée to Mercury as a way of putting an end to such overtures to him!) Platée invites her friends and subjects: "inhabitants of these groves to leave [their] dark marshes" and celebrate life and love with her. The ensuing dance of the marsh creatures is hilarious, accompanied by choruses of cuckoo and frog "*quoi quoi*" sounds from the orchestra. During the dance, Platée is a little put out at the decidedly cool response she receives from Cithéron, who begs her to be calm and to watch as Mercury once more descends from the skies. (18th-century audiences loved all these heavenly ascents and descents in cleverly contrived "machines.") Platée is impressed. Bowing mockingly, Mercury tells her: "The god of thunder, drawn to earth by your beauty, wishes to cast at your feet both his heart and the Universe."

Even Platée is taken aback by this staggering announcement. She gathers herself together, however, and tells Mercury she would welcome a gentle lover, but where is he, this suitor so filled with love? Lightning flashes, cast on the land by the angry Juno. Platée does not fear Juno, she says, because she and her subjects welcome the driving rain in their marsh. Once again the marsh creatures appear and dance grotesquely, parodying the stately court dances to which noble audiences were accustomed. The Aquilons, spirits of the North Winds, rush on to a storm symphony and drive the marsh creatures back to the swamp.

At the start of Act II, Jupiter arrives from on high. Platée is nervous. "Have I the courage to receive his homage?" she asks herself. Jupiter first appears to the frightened frog as a donkey, complete with hee-haw sounds from the orchestra. Then he changes shape and becomes an owl. Platée admires his plumage as he flies away. The crestfallen Platée runs about the stage looking for him. Suddenly there is a clap of thunder. A great shower of gold falls from the skies as Jupiter appears in human form; the god has arrived. He assures Platée that he seeks "naught else but to feel the pleasure of Love." (Jupiter was notorious for his extra-marital liaisons.) Platée is thunder-struck, literally. Jupiter tells her that while they wait for the wedding ceremonies to begin, there will be celebrations. This is an excuse for an extended *divertissement* in which the chorus alternately praises "how beautiful she is" and ridicules her "how droll she is." Platée, who sits in a carriage dressed as a bride, is not quite sure how to react.

The entertainment continues with a stunning *ariette* from La Folie, the personification of folly, who has come to sing and play Apollo's lyre for the dances. This *ariette* parodies the Baroque style in a manner that brings to mind the bravura of Italian arias. La Folie sings of Daphne and Apollo: "Apollo, being smitten with love for Daphne, was yet refused." The dancers mock the unsuspecting Platée. Momus appears, badly disguised as L'Amour, and wishes Platée tears, pain, and weeping. She responds with *"Fie, fie"* and *"Ouffe,"* not exactly the elevated language of French poetry.

Three dancers, a travesty of the Three Graces, appear and dance comically before her. She is disconcerted. The stage fills with more and more people coming to "honor" the frog bride, who is uncertain and confused by all that is happening. Meanwhile, Mercury meets with Juno and tells her to wait nearby until he summons her.

At last it is time for the wedding. Jupiter takes Platée by the hand and begins "I swear..." He holds up the ceremony repeating "I swear" many times, looking anxiously over his shoulder at Mercury; he is waiting for Juno to appear and urges Mercury to hurry her up, saying, "The moment has come to end all this pretense." Then, at last, a raging Juno appears and storms across the stage to put an end to this new affair of her husband. "Stop," she roars, striding up to Platée and tearing the veil from her face. Juno cannot believe what she sees before her and laughs at the frog's terror-stricken face as Jupiter turns to his wife, murmuring, "Can you have any further doubts that I love you?" Platée and her followers run wildly offstage as Jupiter and Juno pledge their love for one another before ascending back to their home on Mount Olympus. "It is no longer meet for the earth to further detain the sovereign of the gods," Jupiter states somewhat pompously, oblivious of the pain he has inflicted on Platée – she is, after all, a mere frog, a nymph from the marshes. The gods leave, disappearing in a great cloud (or not, depending on the production).

Platée is dragged back on stage by the chorus who dance around and make fun of her. She threatens them, impotently, with all kinds of punishment, finally settling on Cithéron as the cause of her downfall, of "this appalling affront." Finally, desperately, she takes a leap into the marsh and disappears. A splash of water is all that remains of the vain, love-struck, abandoned, once bride-to-be, Platée.

So ends the sorry tale of a frog who would marry a god, a humorous yet cruel little tale that, on many levels, parodied the French court with its affectations, the heartlessness of the aristocracy in regard to lesser beings, and the structured, classical style of opera so popular with the courtiers because it glorified themselves. Obvious as all this satire is to us today, it seems to have passed unnoticed by the very people satirized. This was just as well, for if Rameau had been suspected of parodying the king and court, his career would have been over – or worse.

Platée was something entirely new for its time. Rameau was so drawn to Jacques Autreau's poem on which the libretto was based, *"Platée, or the Jealousy of Juno,"* that he bought the rights to the work and gave it to Le Valois d'Orville to fashion into a libretto. Although d'Orville, an accomplished man of letters, did not do justice to the genius of Rameau, the two men did produce a work of buffoonery unlike any other, a *comédie-lyrique* that truly parodied the popular *tragédie-lyrique* style. Both at Versailles and on the stage of the prestigious Académie Royale de Musique, Rameau incorporated, for the first time, such elements of the fairground theatres as a mocking tone, alliteration, comical costumes, slapstick, animal sounds, laughter, and weeping. Even the orchestra joins in the humor with rhythmic vivacity, the use of tambourins, and sudden, unexpected changes in tempi. Platée is described by music; though her appearance is grotesque, her personality is lively. She is changeable; a sensitive, if vain soul one moment, violent and unreasonable the next. The orchestra imitates the sounds of animals and birds, even the braying of a donkey. The false solemnity of some of the dances turns them into burlesques; the endless *chaconne* in the last act is designed to try Platée – and our patience – as the action is drawn out in order to give Juno time to arrive and disrupt the wedding.

La Folie was an entirely new invention with her breezy insolence, her irony, and egotistical self-aggrandizement. She leads the dance before the wedding and exists simply to entertain, to be music. Her *ariette* in the final act is a show-stopper that tests the vocal skills of a flamboyant, yet lyrical soprano. Vocal display, in Rameau, was typically confined to long-held notes without the extreme ornamentation of the Baroque era, although, in the case of La Folie's virtuoso *ariette* "Amour, lance tes traits," (Love, shoot your arrows), there is some humorous parodying of the usual ornamentation.

Rameau filled his score with the airs, recitatives, dances, and choruses one finds in the works of Lully, with their notated declamatory rhythms, an active bass line accompaniment, and frequent changes of metre in the recitatives. Rameau extended these features, giving them a greater sophistication that both enhances and intensifies the vocal line. Rameau's *airs* ranged from very brief *petits airs* to the *air de monologue*, precursor of the aria as we know it today, in which highly charged emotions were expressed at length. His orchestration, which introduced both horns and clarinets, has a symphonic richness that comes to the fore in the dance sequences. Rameau experimented with orchestral techniques; he was, after all, the authority on theory and harmony in his writings at the time. He adapted his ballets to existing dance forms, capturing a wide variety of moods, making explicit in the music the emotions the dancers should express, a boon to the choreographers of his day.

Though comedy often contains a streak of cruelty, such as when we laugh at the misfortunes of others, in *Platée* this aspect of the story is complicated. The *grande dame* of the swamp is to be pitied, maybe even identified with on some level, for comedy works best when one empathizes with the situation or character presented. Platée's treatment at the hands of the gods is inexcusable in any century. The fact that the role is sung by a man takes the edge off the meanness in the plot, but this diva of the swamp, believing herself to be beautiful, does not deserve such heartless treatment.

Even today, the opera *Platée* is a genre all of its own.

It's success in production depends on a superb singing actor to play Platée, as well as singers who understand the Baroque's courtly artifices, and professional dancers. Santa Fe's production will be directed by Frenchman Laurent Pelly, with Laura Scozzi as his choreographer, a pair with a subtle French edge to their humor. The same team directed both Offenbach's hilarious *La Belle Hélène* and Massenet's *Cendrillon* for The Santa Fe Opera in recent years. Platée is sung by Jean-Paul Fouchecourt, who reinvented the role in productions at Covent Garden in London and New York City Opera. Rameau scored the role for a *haute-contre*, a high-pitched tenor (not a countertenor), with a high natural sound. The *haute-contre*, a light tenor with a good balance of registers, was a voice that was very popular in French Baroque opera.

Platée is a gem for its humor and satire, and for its delightful mix of opera and ballet in the French Baroque style of the mid-18th century. In the final analysis, perhaps the moral to be culled from *Platée* is: "Be kind to your web-footed friends, they live all alone in the swamp!"

♪

Characters

Platée, a marsh nymph, a frog	high tenor
Jupiter, god of Olympus	baritone
Juno, wife of Jupiter	mezzo-soprano
Cithéron, king of Mount Cithéron	baritone
Momus, god of ridicule	tenor
La Folie, or Folly	soprano
L'Amour, or Love	soprano
Thalia, muse of comedy	soprano
Mercury, god of skill and dexterity, and Jupiter's messenger	tenor
Thespis, the inventor of comedy	tenor

Bibliography

Grout, Donald Jay. *A Short History of Opera*. New York: Columbia University Press, 1965.

Platée, Libretto and Liner Notes, CD: Musifrance Erato-Disques 2292-45028-2, 1998.

Sadie, Stanley, ed. *The New Grove Dictionary of Opera*, vol. 3. London: Macmillan Reference Ltd., 1992.

Don Alfonso

Così fan tutte

Wolfgang Amadeus Mozart

Così fan tutte has always been an enigmatic opera, reams have been written about it in the effort to analyze, dissect and explain Mozart's intentions. Maybe, just maybe, Mozart wanted *Così* to be simply a light-hearted comedy on the amusing subject of partner-swapping. At this point in his career, in 1789, Mozart had completed *Don Giovanni*, was living in Vienna and struggling to survive financially. He had less than two years to live; following *Così fan tutte*, he would write only two more operas, *La clemenza di Tito* and *Die Zauberflöte* before his untimely death.

Two of the six people we meet in the opera are sisters from Ferrara who are staying (for reasons undisclosed) on their own in a villa by the Bay of Naples in full sight of the volatile Vesuvius. Mozart set the opera in his own time just after the French Revolution when Europe was in a state of vast social upheaval. Yet in this idyllic spot, little disturbed the peace and languor of sun-filled days.

The sisters, Dorabella and Fiordiligi, are completely in love with their eminently suitable suitors, the handsome military officers Ferrando and Guglielmo. They gaze longingly at the images of their fiancés in miniature portraits they wear round their necks. In an almost overly sweet duet, they sing of their lovers' virtues: "This is Adonis/Apollo, more lovely in Nature than Art, no aspect is wanting in this warrior/lover." The girls sigh in a broken rhythmic pattern suggesting lovesickness. They are young and in love – what could possibly happen to darken their days? Their days are darkened and their happiness is undone by Don Alfonso, an older friend of the two officers who would be the young men's mentor, guiding them in the ways of the world, and particularly in the ways of women.

Mozart departs from operatic tradition by opening *Così fan tutte* with a series of trios when the three men meet in a coffee shop. The officers affirm their faith and trust in the constancy of their fiancées while Don Alfonso aggravates them by asking, "Are these two creatures goddesses or are they women, no more, no less?" He tries to reason with his young friends on the subject of women's constancy, but his words fall on deaf ears. The cynical older man has little faith in women and no time for "blushes, sighs, and palpitations." Is it not time to take Dorabella and Fiordiligi down from their lofty pedestals and test the love they proclaim so vehemently? He good-humoredly proposes a wager of a hundred guineas that the girls, when tempted, will be unfaithful. Ferrando and Guglielmo, in a teasing dotted rhythm, are scornful at first of Don Alfonso's proposal but later jump at the chance to prove their fiancées' constancy and win the bet. They plan, then and there, to throw a big party. These are not sophisticated lovers; they, like the girls, are of the bourgeoisie, and up to this point, life has been good to all of them.

The test begins when, accompanied by syncopated strings that describe his pretended agitation, Don Alfonso tells the girls that their fiancés have been called to war and must leave at once – this is the first deceit. His news leads to a tearful quintet in which the lovers bid one another tender farewells as Alfonso chuckles to the audience from the side of the stage. Martial music summons the men away, and Alfonso is left with the two girls to sing a hauntingly beautiful trio, "Soave sia il vento" (O wind gently blowing), in which they pray that the young men will be safe. Listen for the gentle harmonies and the soft string accompaniment in the trio. This exquisite prayer, based on a charade, is the first of many intriguing ambiguities that Mozart and his librettist, Lorenzo da Ponte, weave into the plot. In *Così* it is far from clear when the characters are serious and when they are parodying either themselves, a given situation, or opera itself. Mozart's own position is ambiguous, generously allowing interpretative scope to singers and directors. The music, however, implies that Mozart is firmly on the side of the girls, while the words tell us that da Ponte, in his pointed libretto, leans towards skepticism.

Da Ponte had personal reasons for his cynical approach to the subject matter, for his mistress at the time, a tempestuous soprano called La Ferrarese, was rumored to have been involved in a partner-swapping scandal thus inadvertently providing the poet with many ideas for the plot. Da Ponte encouraged Mozart to give the role of Fiordiligi to La Ferrarese. While not especially impressed with his friend's mistress, Mozart agreed, and composed the most challenging arias of heroic leaps and falls for her voice.

The mood of farewell which concludes the first scene changes abruptly as Despina, the girls' maid, complains of her lot in life as she samples the hot chocolate she has just prepared for her mistresses. In Despina we meet the opera's sixth and final principal character. The musical and dramatic action concerns itself with the play and interplay of the three pairs: Dorabella and Ferrando, Fiordiligi and Guglielmo, Don Alfonso and Despina, who together form a natural symmetry in the classical style. For now, however, the men momentarily leave the stage, supposedly to go to war, as the women are left alone, sadly entwining arms and comforting one another.

Bereft and distraught at the departure of their lovers, Despina's mistresses are in no mood for chocolate. Their maid laughs at their distress. In a flurry of bright patter and repeated notes, Despina points out that men, especially soldiers, are not expected to be faithful and, should they not return, "There's plenty more to choose from." In a line that 18th-century audiences loved because of its innuendo, Despina assures the sisters "Di pasta simile" (Men are like pasta) suggesting all men are made from the same stuff – pasta! There is a sense of tit for tat happening here: if women are viewed as inconstant and fickle, then maybe men are also, (like pasta), changeable, flexible, even wilting!

When the girls flounce off to their rooms, Don Alfonso takes Despina aside and offers her a gold coin if she will help him introduce two new suitors to the sisters. As cynical as he, Despina agrees at once to be his accomplice, and Alfonso ushers in two young men dressed as Albanian officers. This is the second lie for the two are, of course, Ferrando and Guglielmo. Alfonso uses Despina to test their disguises. Needing her as an ally, he only tells her half the truth. Despina doesn't recognize the "Albanians" and, when the girls enter, she watches delightedly as the two strangers in exotic costumes profess their love for the sisters who are highly insulted and offended at their effrontery. When Don Alfonso arrives a few moments later, he explains that the men are his friends and, like a puppet master, begins to direct the girls to new partners.

The individual characters of the four principals, hinted at in the opening scenes, now begin to emerge more clearly. In their first scenes, the sisters express identical sentiments and feelings – they come as a pair, they even sing in thirds and sixths. But when faced with decisions for which there are no clear guidelines, they react differently. In an astonishing coloratura aria "Come scoglio immoto resta" (As a rock remains unmoved), Fiordiligi states that she will stand firm like a rock in the ocean against the advances of any man. This vocal extravaganza borders on parody while challenging the range and pyrotechnics of the best singers. Of the two sisters, Fiordiligi is serious and rational, more likely to follow the rules of reason, though even she admits, at the start of the opera, that she is restless for adventure. The spontaneous Dorabella is more likely to follow the dictates of her heart.

Guglielmo pleads the Albanians' cause in his aria, but the girls continue to insist that the men leave. Once alone, the men congratulate themselves that their fiancées have stood the test of constancy so well, and demand their winnings. "Not so fast," Alfonso says, "It's not over yet." Guglielmo is pragmatic and self-assured, while Ferrando sings of love in a meltingly lovely aria, "Un'aura amorosa" (An amorous breath). By the end of the opera, Ferrando will discover unanticipated feelings of anger within himself when he learns that his Dorabella is human, "no more, no less," and will say, "The voice of reason is overwhelmed by the conflicting urges of passion!"

In the finale of Act I, the "problems in petticoats," the "unassailable rocks," are under siege. The Albanians stagger into the garden of the villa where they pretend to drink arsenic in full sight of Dorabella and Fiordiligi before falling to the ground. This ploy catches the girls off guard, but instinct demands that they rush to the aid of the fallen men. As Dorabella approaches, she admits "They've a certain strange attraction." In a hilarious scene straight out of *commedia dell'arte*, Don Alfonso announces the arrival of Doctor Mesmer (Despina in disguise) – then all the rage in Vienna for his cures with his "mesmerizing" magnet.

Anton Mesmer, the father of hypnotism, believed that an "animal magnetism" drew people together, and that this magnetism accounted for man's social instincts and was the reason and motivation behind human behavior.

He also explored mysticism and the occult, both of which were popular in Europe at the time. Later, his studies and treatments of psychosexual effects eventually discredited him in Vienna. Mozart, poking gentle fun at Mesmer in this funny topical scene, owed much to the doctor, who had presented the young composer's one-act pastorale or *Singspiel, Bastien und Bastienne*, in the garden of his Viennese home many years before, when Mozart was only twelve.

As the "doctor," Despina draws a magnet up and down the bodies of the men, removing "negative essences." The Albanians slowly recover and, predictably enough, ask for a kiss from the hovering girls to complete their "cure." The couples, aware now of subtle change, negative essences notwithstanding, are unsure how to proceed as the normal social patterns begin to fall away. The scene ends with a lively sextet: the girls try to stand firm against new and unsettling feelings, the men celebrate the girls' perceived constancy, as Alfonso and Despina comment, "Men desiring, girls refusing, nothing could be more confusing," in the first act's classic Mozartean finale.

Act II opens with Despina's lecture to her mistresses on how to act as women: "By treating love as a diversion, never miss your chances." Dorabella, beginning to change her mind, suggests to her sister that a mild flirtation could do no harm; "We only seek diversion to ward off melancholy and boredom." Fiordiligi is not so sure, but when Dorabella takes the initiative by deciding to flirt with the dark one (who is not her fiancé), Fiordiligi agrees to "take the fair one, and the comedy begins." In the course of this discussion the girls work themselves up into a state of enthusiasm as one sings over the other and the duet ends, not with one, but with a series of cadences that underline the girls' intoxication with their own idea.

The men arrive in a boat to serenade the girls, and the

seduction gets underway in earnest. Choreographed by Alfonso and Despina, the four young people pair up and walk together in different sections of the garden. The flirtation between Dorabella and Guglielmo ends when Guglielmo succeeds in getting Dorabella's locket from her in exchange for a pendant heart he gives her. Dorabella's own heart beats a little faster at the proximity of the attractive Albanian: "I feel like Vesuvius erupting inside," she says as she waltzes off into a shadowed arbor with her new partner.

Fiordiligi, on the other hand, continues to resist the advances of the gallant Ferrando; she is having a difficult time with her conscience. She sings the magnificent "Per pietà, ben mio" (Have pity, my love). This aria has a clear melodic line with great leaps of an octave and a half; the horns and woodwind are well to the fore in the orchestra, with elaborate comments from the woodwinds as the aria ends. Fiordiligi keeps Ferrando at arm's length, though when he leaves she admits to herself that she is smitten. When the men meet to compare notes, Ferrando is furious to hear Guglielmo boast that Dorabella has succumbed to him; he has not had the same success with Fiordiligi. More firmly resolved than ever to break her resistance, Ferrando returns with impassioned words of love and Fiordiligi also surrenders. The men now find themselves in an unexpected dilemma: they never dreamed the girls would be untrue, but they still love them. Jealous and unsure, they don't know what to do. Don Alfonso tells them they have nothing to lose, reasoning that if Dorabella and Fiordiligi are untrue, then probably *all* women are untrue, so they may as well marry their erring fiancées as originally planned. "Così fan tutte" (All women are like that) they sing, it's the way of human nature; the girls must be accepted as they are. The materialistic Alfonso, a man of reason, suggests that human beings generally follow their natural inclinations, and that women are as amenable to being seduced as men are to seduce. Again Mozart, in the words of Don Alfonso, seems to be arguing that men and women are equal, if only in their susceptibility to seduction.

The disgruntled men agree to a mock double wedding, with Despina acting as the notary. An instant wedding is prepared. The Albanians and the sisters sing together in such a way that it is impossible to tell who is addressing whom – do the men sing to their original loves or to the new ones? Despina arrives, disguised as the notary, and the ceremony begins. The girls have just signed the wedding papers when the sound of drums and singing is heard in the distance. The soldiers are returning! Terrified of what will happen, the girls panic. They push the Albanians out of sight and moments later, lo and behold, their own Ferrando and Guglielmo appear in military cloaks. To their pretended horror, the returning officers learn that, in their absence, the girls were about to marry other men. Despina is unmasked. Alfonso tells the men that all the proof they need is in the next room. The men rush off, only to return moments later wearing part of their Albanian costumes and singing once again their lines of seduction to the devastated girls.

The action stalls until Don Alfonso comes forward and admits that the charade was all his doing. His plan was to teach the young people a lesson: "Nothing's perfect here below." He suggests they forgive one another and laugh the matter off "For there is nothing else to do." The chastened couples take one another's hands as Despina, the know-it-all maid remarks, "Take good care if fooling others; someone else may well fool you." So ends *Così* and we leave the theatre happy, but a little uncertain about the outcome of the plot.

There are myriad ways of interpreting *Così*. Maybe Fiordiligi and Dorabella, two girls from Ferrara, who arrived in Naples and settled into a villa all on their own, were just out for a good time with an eye to making an advantageous catch in terms of a husband. They arrive at the villa with no family, no chaperons, no male protectors, but they do seem to have live-in boyfriends, for the officers' clothes, we are told, were hanging in the villa's closet. Maybe we should not be taken in by the Jane Austen-ish façade of the sisters. These two girls fall in love as easily with exotic Albanians as they do with their own young, good-looking officers.

The girls play their parts to perfection registering hysteria when their lovers go off to war, then rapidly drying their tears and falling in love all over again when the Albanians appear. Despina, their street-wise servant, knows their tricks and is not impressed. Despina does, however, readily enter into the plot to deceive her mistresses when Don Alfonso, the puppeteer who masterminds the plot, is prepared to pay her in gold for her efforts. When the worldly-wise Don Alfonso suggests the ploy to test the girls' constancy, he too is game-playing.

These six characters are bored with little to do during long, indolent days spent on the beach at Naples. No wonder they dream up some diversion to pass the time. Partner-swapping might liven things up, Don Alfonso thinks, especially when the girls are not let in on the secret that the Albanians are in fact their officers in disguise – 18th-century audiences reveled in such disguises. Such a plot would provide an amusing evening's entertainment, and keep boredom at bay. The idea of partner-swapping was hardly new; the Greeks wrote about it, and it still happens today.

The question of what is real and what illusion is always asked in connection with *Così*. Some authors argue at length that the real love relationships in the opera exist in the original pairings with the swap merely a game to test the waters, to see how far the girls (and the men) will go and what lessons are to be learned before reverting back to the status quo. Others argue, equally forcibly, that the happy involvement of the engaged couples is an illusion; such relationships are socially acceptable making for appropriate marriages, but without a deep, abiding love being part of the equation. It is when the girls meet strange men who are not part of their social milieu, that they let their hearts and feelings guide them, rather than following a set of prescribed social manners. It is in these circumstances, it is argued, that the girls fall in love, and are true to themselves and their new lovers.

That the opera starts and ends in the key of C major suggests that Mozart and da Ponte intended to bring the opera full circle – in the end little has changed. "Let's laugh it off and forget about it," Don Alfonso says. Forget the joke and head to the beach for another lazy day in the sun as if nothing had happened. But everything has changed, there is a loss of innocence and trust, the four young people cannot go back to the carefree existence they once led. Herein lies the uncertainty and the enigma one feels about this opera.

Directors have a hey day with *Così*. The traditional ending indicates that the girls are restored to their original partners, having been suitably chastened after being found out, not just for flirting, but actually planning to marry strangers. In today's productions, the girls may indeed end up with their new partners, truly in love and not bowing to social pressure. Or the ending may be left up in the air as when the four principals stand in line at the end holding hands with no indication as to who "belongs" to whom. One contemporary production ended with the girls storming off the stage in a huff in one direction, as the two men leave hand in hand in the other.

That people, managements, critics and audiences alike, have been unsettled by this opera over the years is clear from the many titles inflicted on it: *Love and Temptation* (Frankfurt, 1791), *The Wager or Maidenly Love* (Stuttgart, 1796), *Tit for Tat or The Tables Turned* (London, 1828). It was said that Beethoven took the immorality of *Così* so seriously that he wrote a corrective eulogy about women's constancy as a rebuttal in *Fidelio*, when Leonora, the faithful wife, sings, "O Komm... Hoffnung!" (O come... Hope). As in Mozart's aria "Per pieta" for Fiordiligi, Beethoven used the same key of E major, obbligato horns, heroic arpeggios and the same huge downward leap from high G sharp.

Mozart's title, *Così fan tutte*, actually comes from a line in his own *Marriage of Figaro* when Don Basilio comments, on finding Cherubino and the gardener's daughter in one another's arms, "Così fan tutte le belle" (That's what all pretty girls do). The little musical phrase that accompanies these words is played many, many times in the overture of the opera, *Così*. While offensive as this line is perceived to be in our time, *Così* could also be interpreted as "women are a challenge, with minds of their own, imponderable forces, mysteries." This interpretation is much more in line with Mozart's approach to women in most of his operas. The whole problem of the title could have been resolved if Mozart and da Ponte had changed one letter, making *tutte*, meaning women, to *tutti*, meaning all people.

Mozart was under a lot of pressure when he composed *Così*. He and his wife Constanze were at the seven year mark in their marriage; neither was in good health. Constanze went to Baden for a cure while her husband struggled to survive in Vienna. The Emperor only asked Mozart to compose music for court balls and paid him little. He had few students. Reports of Constanze's flirtations in Baden came to Mozart's ears and he wrote begging her to behave herself. But he too was having a flirtation. So the marriage was under some stress when Mozart came to write *Così*. This perhaps accounts for many of the very beautiful moments of both anguish and tenderness in the opera.

So maybe *Così* should be enjoyed for its light-hearted plot and for the glory of its music. As to which sister ends up with which man is really immaterial. When Mozart describes love in Ferrando's glowing aria "Un'aura amoroso," or anguish in the real pain Fiordiligi feels when she is torn between being faithful to her old love while being drawn in her heart to a new love – this is what matters. The genius of *Così* lies in its music.

Sitting in the open air at The Santa Fe Opera listening to the first act trio "Soave sia il vento" one may wonder about what is real and what illusion; one may even leave the theatre at the end of the evening changed by the realization that just possibly the reality is Mozart, and the rest, all of it, is illusion. Just allowing oneself to enjoy the spirit of Mozart's music – that is what matters.

Characters

Fiordiligi	{sisters from Ferrara	soprano
Dorabella	living in Naples}	mezzo-soprano
Ferrando, Dorabella's lover		baritone
Guglielmo, Fiordiligi's lover		tenor
Don Alfonso, a philosopher		bass
Despina, a maid		soprano

Bibliography

Brophy, Brigid, *Mozart the Dramatist*, Harcourt, Brace & World Inc., New York, 1964.

Osborne, Charles, *The Complete Operas of Mozart*, Da Capo Press, New York, 1978.

Till, Nicholas, *Mozart and the Enlightenment*, W.W. Norton & Co., New York, 1992.